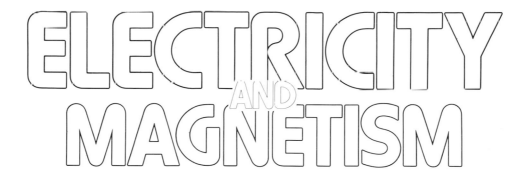

| Design | Cooper · West |
| Editor | Margaret Fagan |
| Researcher | Cecilia Weston-Baker |
| Consultant | Dr. J. W. Warren |
| Illustrators | Louise Nevett |
| | Rob Shone |

First published in
Great Britain in 1985 by
Franklin Watts
12a Golden Square
London W1

First published in the
United States in 1986 by
Gloucester Press

Copyright © Aladdin Books Ltd 1985

Printed in Belgium

ISBN 0-531-17020-9

Library of Congress Catalog
Card Number: 85-81664

# ELECTRICITY AND MAGNETISM

## Kathryn Whyman

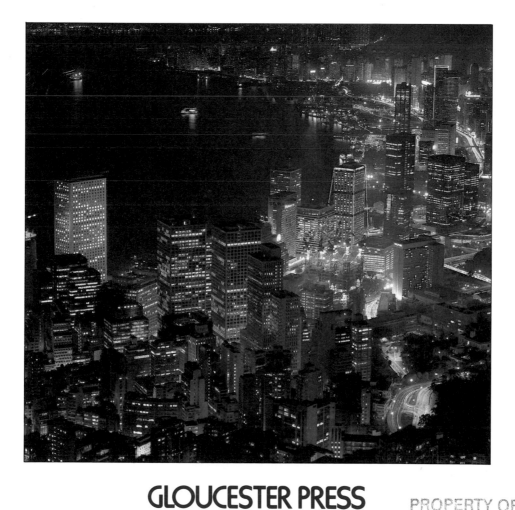

### GLOUCESTER PRESS
New York · Toronto · 1986

# INTRODUCTION

Telephones, stereo systems and video recorders all rely on the power of electricity and magnetism to make them work. Yet many of the electrical devices that we depend on have only been invented in the last fifty years. In fact, people often think of electricity itself as an invention, something "manmade." But electricity occurs in nature in a wide variety of forms. Lightning, electric fish, the Northern Lights, magnetic rocks and the sending of electrical signals in the human brain are just a few examples.

This book looks at how electricity and magnetism are closely related. It explains how together they produce the electric current that we use every day to provide heat, light and power.

# CONTENTS

**Warning**
Electricity can be dangerous. The illustrations and projects in this book are not experiments. Do not touch or play with electric power supply and wires.

# A WORLD WITHOUT ELECTRICITY?

Many parts of the world still do not enjoy a constant and everyday supply of electricity. Yet most of us simply take it for granted, turning switches on and off to power our televisions and washing machines.

It is hard for many of us to imagine a world without an electricity supply. But only a hundred years ago, people used gas and oil or even candles to light their homes. And before the Industrial Revolution, essential supplies such as water had to be transported by hand or beast. All communications were by word of mouth or by mail. Many people still live in this way, but it is not the world most of us know.

Today, whether for survival, to save time or for entertainment, an electricity supply is an essential part of everyday life.

Life without an electricity supply – washing clothes by hand

Hong Kong ablaze with electric light

# ELECTRICITY OCCURS NATURALLY

Electricity occurs naturally when you rub certain materials together. For example, rubbing a blown-up balloon against a sweater makes a type of electricity, or *electric charge*, called "static electricity." The balloon can now pull things toward itself, such as pieces of paper or a thin stream of water from a faucet.

The most dramatic example of electricity occurs naturally when lightning strikes. A flash of lightning is caused by huge amounts of electric charge jumping through the air from cloud to cloud, or to the Earth. This electric charge builds up when small drops of water hit against hailstones in the clouds. Lightning is tremendously powerful – one flash can be seen for many miles and can destroy trees, start fires, damage buildings and kill people.

Sparks of static electricity

**Static electricity**
The faint crackling noise you hear when you take off a sweater or comb your hair is due to tiny sparks of electric charge jumping through the air. As long as the charge remains on the sweater, it can attract hair or small pieces of lint. If you look in the mirror, you may just see how your hair is being made to stand on end!

Forked lightning leaps through the sky to Earth

# THE MAGNETIC EARTH

Two thousand years ago, the Chinese discovered a special black stone. When a small splinter of this stone was allowed to hang by a thread, it always pointed in the same direction. We call this kind of stone "lodestone," and the direction it points is always north-south.

Anything that behaves in the same way as a lodestone is called a magnet. A compass needle is simply a tiny magnet. All magnets exert a force around them, and their lines of force make up a "magnetic field." The Earth itself is like a giant magnet and is also surrounded by its own magnetic field.

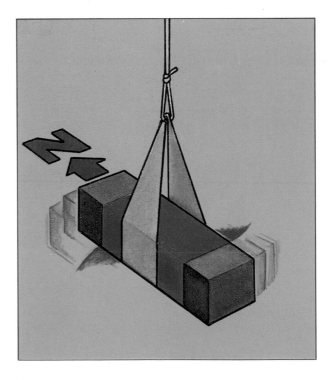

**Magnetic fields**
The magnetism of the Earth is shown as lines of force making up its magnetic field. These lines are drawn between the North Pole and the South Pole.

The end of the magnet which points toward the Earth's North Pole is also called the north pole of the magnet. The other end is called the south pole of the magnet.

Using a map and compass to find the way

A map is very useful to a traveler but it does not tell you in which direction you are facing. You can find this out by using a compass. The compass needle is affected by the Earth's magnetic field and always points northward. The map can then be lined up with the compass. In fact, a compass needle does not point to the geographical or true North Pole. It points to the magnetic north, a point in Northern Canada, 1,000 miles away from the true North Pole.

11

Pointing to the north is only one of the many things a magnet can do. Magnets exert a force on almost anything in their magnetic field. Usually, this force is very weak. But if two magnets are held together so that the north pole of one faces the south pole of the other, you will be able to feel the magnets pulling toward each other until they click together.

Making a magnet is actually very simple. A piece of steel can be easily magnetized by stroking it several times in the same direction with a magnet. A steel magnet is called a "permanent" magnet because it can often keep its magnetic powers for a long time.

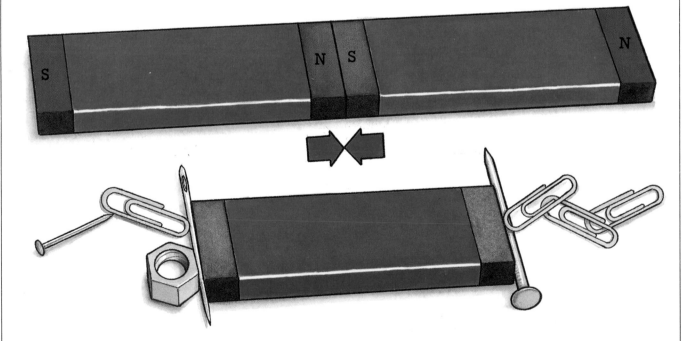

**Attracting opposite poles**
The north and south poles of a magnet are described as opposite poles. If opposite poles of two magnets are placed near each other they *attract*.

**Attracting metals**
Small iron or steel objects, like pins and paper clips, will be attracted to the magnet. This attraction is strongest at each of the magnet's poles.

# MAGNETIC HOVERING TRAINS

Magnets have another interesting property. If they are held so that like poles are facing, they will push each other away or *repel*. This principle can be seen at work in a special magnetic hovering train. Powerful magnets placed beneath the train all have their north poles facing down toward the track. The track is also unusual as it too acts as a magnet.

These magnets have their north poles facing up toward the train. Because the north poles repel each other, the train is lifted off the track. It can now glide along the track with ease. The magnets used by the magnetic train are not permanent – they only attract and repel when electricity flows through them. Magnets like these are called "electromagnets."

A magnetic hovering train in Japan

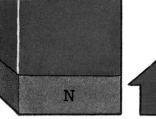

Like poles repel

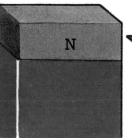

# ELECTROMAGNETS

Electricity and magnetism are very closely related. In fact, another way of making a magnet is to pass electricity through a wire wrapped around a metal core, usually iron. The iron core becomes an "electromagnet" like the ones in the magnetic train. Smaller electromagnets are used everyday in the home; look inside an electric doorbell and you will probably see an electromagnet shaped like a horse-shoe with coils of wire wrapped around its arms.

Powerful electromagnets are often to be seen at work in junkyards. Because magnets only attract a few metals, they can be used to separate one kind of metal from another. Some electromagnets are even strong enough to lift several tons of scrap iron or steel girders.

**A simple electromagnet**
When electricity flows through the wire, the nail, now an electromagnet, can pick up paper clips. An electromagnet is not a permanent magnet – once the iron core loses its magnetism the paper clips drop.

Iron nail

Wire wrapped around the nail

Battery

Paper clips

15

An electromagnetic crane used to lift scrap iron and steel

# MAKING AN ELECTRIC CURRENT

We have seen that electricity occurs naturally as static electricity. But static electricity is the sudden and uncontrollable movement of an electric charge, so it cannot be used very easily to drive machines. Instead, many machines are driven by an "electric current," which is *the controlled movement of an electric charge.*

Not only can electricity make magnets, but magnets can also make, or "generate," an electric current! A bicycle "dynamo" is a simple device that generates enough electric current to light up a bicycle's lights. In some rural places, people use a gasoline or diesel engine to drive a powerful kind of dynamo called a "generator," to provide their own source of electric current.

An electric current can be made to flow through a wire, by moving the wire across a magnetic field. It does not matter if the wire or the magnet moves, as long as one moves in relation to the other. A bicycle dynamo produces an electric current by using the movement of the wheel to move a magnet within a coil of wire.

Small light bulb

Magnet

Loop of wire

Turning power

A simple dynamo

A small, local generator in China

# THE POWER STATION

Power stations produce electricity on a large scale, for factories, cities and homes. They use giant generators, usually powered by coal, gas, oil or the energy from nuclear reactions. In these cases, steam is produced at great pressure to drive the "turbine." The turbine is like a series of huge wheels or fans with many blades and it is spun around by the force of the steam. In a hydroelectric power station, the force of moving water turns the turbine instead of steam. The turbine, in turn, drives the generator.

There are many different types of generators powered by a variety of sources; but in all of them the electric current is generated by magnets being turned quickly inside coils of wire.

The familiar sight of cooling towers at a power station

18

A series of turbine blades and the generator under construction

# FROM POWER STATION TO HOME

Once the electric current has been generated, it must be carried from the power station to wherever it is needed. Electric current is carried in thick wires known as cables. Some are buried beneath the ground and others, supported by pylons, are carried high above the ground.

A system of pylons and cables connects all the power stations in the country into one huge network called the "grid." The grid network allows power to be switched from one area to another, as demand for the current varies. Even if a power station fails, a local power cut can still be avoided. Electric current from another power station is simply sent along the cables to maintain the power supply in the area.

Pylons carrying cables from the power station

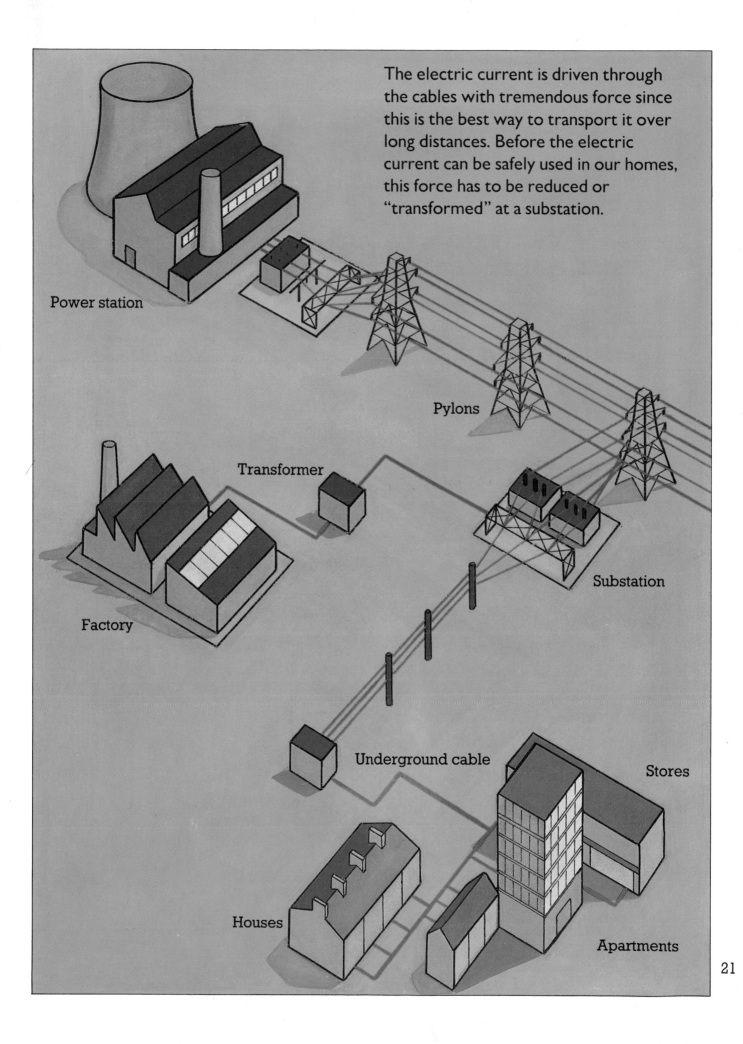

The electric current is driven through the cables with tremendous force since this is the best way to transport it over long distances. Before the electric current can be safely used in our homes, this force has to be reduced or "transformed" at a substation.

Power station

Pylons

Transformer

Factory

Substation

Underground cable

Stores

Houses

Apartments

# ELECTRICITY TRAVELS IN CIRCUITS

To connect a light bulb to an electricity supply we need two wires. Electric current flows from the power supply, down one wire to the bulb and back along the other wire to the power supply. The path of the electric current is called a "circuit." As long as there are no breaks in the circuit, the current will continue to flow and the bulb will stay lit. But if the circuit is broken, the bulb will immediately go out.

Most electric wires are made of thin metal strands covered with a plastic or rubber coating. The electric current can flow easily through the metal strands but not through the plastic. When the current flows through the wire, the wire becomes *live*. For safety, electric plugs are made of plastic and in some countries they are fitted with a fuse.

### A simple circuit

A switch is simply a way of making and breaking a circuit. When a switch is in the "on" position, an electric current flows through the circuit. As soon as the switch is turned to the "off" position, the circuit is broken.

Paper clip

Switch in "off" position

Thumbtacks

A faulty wire can produce enough heat to start a house fire

If the wires leading to and from a light bulb touch each other, there is a sudden increase in current flowing through them and they become very hot. This is called a "short circuit" and can be a fire risk.

To avoid this fire risk, many plugs or circuits are fitted with a fuse — a piece of wire in a circuit that melts as soon as the current is too high. Once the fuse "blows," the circuit is broken.

Fuse

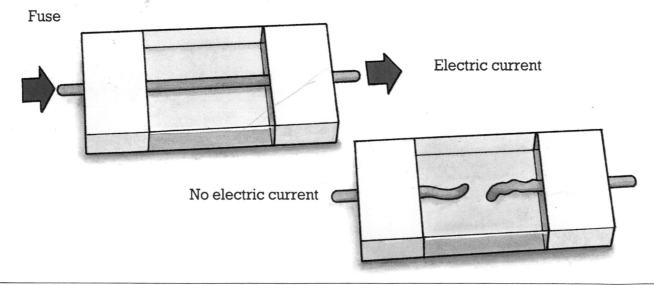

Electric current

No electric current

23

# SO WHAT IS AN ELECTRIC CURRENT?

A wire is made up of millions of particles much too small to see. These particles are called atoms. Even the tiny atom itself is made up of several different parts. Around the center of the atom, the "nucleus," particles called "electrons" are arranged. These electrons circle around the nucleus at different distances from it and at great speed.

An atom consists of a nucleus surrounded by electrons moving in orbits. Each electron is a tiny negative charge and is attracted to the positively charged nucleus.

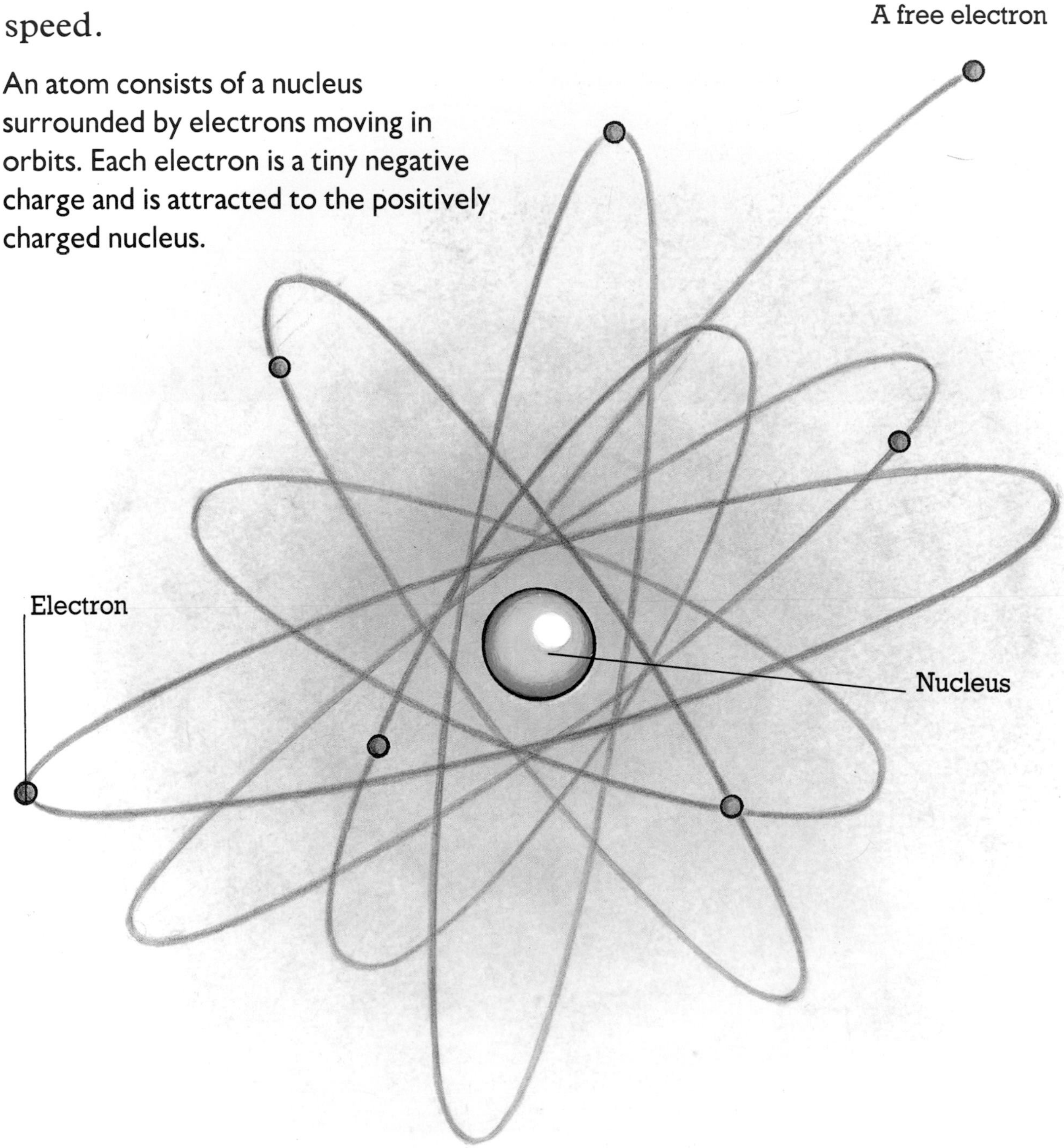

A free electron

Electron

Nucleus

In a metal wire, however, the outer electrons are free to wander at random around the atoms. When a wire is connected to a power supply, like a battery, these free outer electrons are driven in a single direction. Each electron is, in fact, a tiny negative charge and it is this flow of negative charge which we call an electric current. To make a flashlight bulb light up for one second takes a flow of about one million, million, million electrons!

When an electric current flows, the free outer electrons all move in the same direction. In the very thin wire in a light bulb, the filament, the collisions between the electrons and atoms are more frequent than in an ordinary wire. This increases the temperature of the wire and makes the wire give off heat, which we see as light.

Filament

# BATTERIES

Flashlights, alarm clocks and many other portable appliances need their own power supply and they use batteries. A battery cannot store electricity but is used to make an electric current when it is needed. Inside the battery there are two metal plates, each covered by a special chemical. When the battery is connected to a light bulb in a circuit, a stream of electrons flows through the chemical from one plate to the other, along the wire, and lights up the bulb.

Batteries come in many different shapes and sizes depending on what they are needed for. Many have to be thrown away once the chemicals have been used up but others can be "recharged" and so may last a very long time.

A battery can be large enough to power a car, or small enough to fit into a radio

# THE ELECTRIC MOTOR

Toy cars are often powered by an electric motor connected to a battery. An electric motor depends on the same principle as a dynamo: the movement of a wire coil in a magnetic field. In the dynamo, a turning force is used to generate an electric current. However, in the electric motor, a current is used to produce a turning force which drives a shaft connected to the wheels of a car.

Turning power

Electric motor

Toy cars are often powered by batteries

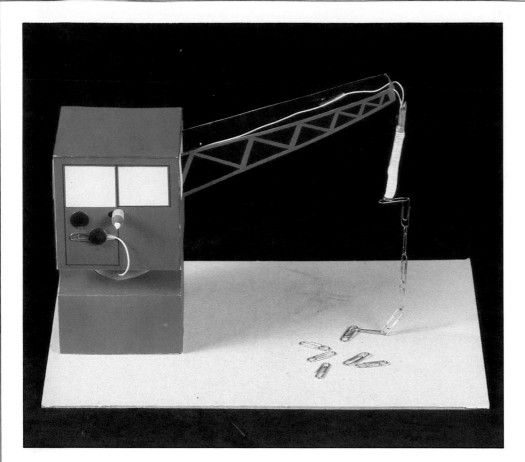

By following the instructions and diagrams, you can make your own electromagnetic crane. You can use it to pick up small metal objects.

### What You Need
An iron nail, a yard of thin plastic coated wire, two boxes, a spool, a pencil, a 1.5v battery, a cardboard tube, some cardboard, two thumbtacks, a paper clip, some glue and adhesive tape, and scissors.

### Making the Electromagnet
Wind the middle part of the wire tightly round the nail, leaving the ends free. One end should be about eight inches longer than the other. When the ends of the wire are connected to the battery the nail should become a magnet.

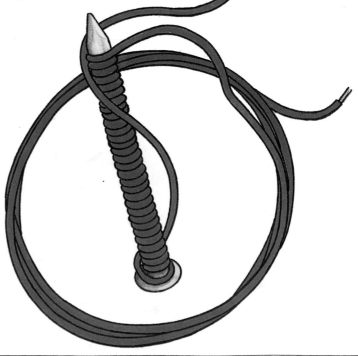

28

## Making the Crane

Make the arm by folding a piece of cardboard. Pierce two holes in the end of it. Glue the base of the arm to a spool. Push a pencil through the cardboard and the spool. Remove the pencil and place the spool halfway down the upper box. Make holes in this box for the pencil. Now make slits so the arm can move up and down.

Cut a hole in the top of the lower box, big enough to fit the tube into. Cut a smaller hole in the bottom of the upper box and fix the tube as shown.

## Wiring

Push two thumbtacks into the upper box. One should hold a paper clip in position. This acts as a switch. Cut a piece of wire six inches long from the long end of wire attached to the nail. All the ends of the wires should have their plastic coating removed. Connect up the wires with tape as shown in the diagram. Decorate your crane as you choose. When the clip touches both tacks, the crane will be ready to use.

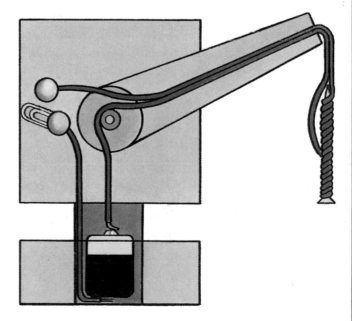

29

# MORE ABOUT ELECTRICITY

## Measuring an electric current

We can measure how much current is moving through a wire by using an ammeter. An ammeter is rather like a traffic census counting the number of vehicles driving past a given point on a road. We measure the flow of electrons in amperes (AMPS). If the current measures one amp, it means that six million million million electrons flow past a single point in the wire each second.

## Measuring voltage

The negative terminal of the battery may be very negative in respect to the positive terminal. In this case, electrons are pushed along the wire very hard. We say that the electric current flows with a high voltage. If the negative terminal is weaker, the electrons are pushed more gently. The electric current now has a low voltage. Voltage is measured in units called VOLTS by a voltmeter.

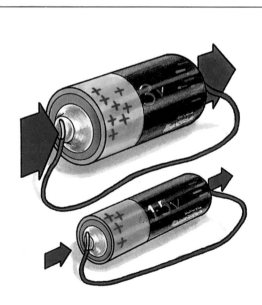

## Watts

If you look on a light bulb, you will see another measurement. These are WATTS, a unit of power. The power of electricity depends on how much current is flowing (its amps) and how hard it is being pushed (its volts). The faster it moves and the harder it is pushed, the greater the power.

# GLOSSARY

### Atom
Every substance is made up of atoms which are themselves made up of a central nucleus surrounded by tiny moving electrons. The nucleus consists of two main kinds of particles, protons and neutrons.

### Electric charge
The particles of an atom carry electric charge. Particles inside the nucleus (protons) each carry a positive charge. Neutrons have no electrical charge attached to them. When there is an equal number of electrons and protons, the atom itself has no overall charge. If any electrons (negative charges) move away from the atom, the atom is left positively charged. If more electrons are gained by an atom, it becomes negatively charged. Positive and negative charges *attract* each other, but like charges, for example two electrons, *repel*.

### Electric current
A flow of electrons (negative charges) around a circuit.

### Lines of force
The force of a magnet is exerted along lines. These lines extend from the north to the south pole, all around the magnet. Together, these lines of force make up the magnetic field.

### Orbit
The path taken by an electron as it circles around the nucleus of an atom.

### Recharge
To build up charge again once it has been lost. Car batteries, for example, can be recharged once they have gone "flat."

### Static electricity
When certain materials are rubbed together, electrons move from one material to the other. The substance losing electrons becomes positively charged while the substance gaining electrons gains a negative charge. As opposite charges attract, the two materials, such as a balloon and your hair, "stick" together. Once the electrons have built up on one material they do not flow, so this form of electricity is called "static electricity." If the build-up of electrons is great enough, however, they may leap across to the positively charged material as a spark. The static electricity is then discharged.

### Substation
Electricity leaves the power station at very high voltages. This is gradually reduced at substations. The electric current may pass through several substations before finally entering your home at the correct voltage.

# INDEX

**Photographic Credits:**
Cover, Zefa; title, Spectrum; contents,
Picturepoint; page 6, Zefa; page 7,
Spectrum; page 9, Zefa; page 11,
Barnaby's; page 13, Tony Stone; page 15,
Barnaby's; page 17, Peter Fraenkel; page
18, Tony Stone; page 19, CEGB; page 20,
Tony Stone; page 23, Zefa; page 26,
Spectrum; page 27, Robert Harding;
page 28, Stephen Sandon.

PRINTED IN BELGIUM BY
proost
INTERNATIONAL BOOK PRODUCTION